POLAR REGION
ACTIVITY BOOK
Explore The Arctic and Antarctic Through Arts & Crafts

Written by Mary Jo Keller

Edited by Kathy Rogers

Design by Pete Brower

Illustrated by Barb Lorseyedi

About the Author

Mary Jo Keller attended The College of New Rochelle in New Rochelle, New York and William and Mary in Williamsburg.

For the past fifteen years she has designed and implemented programs for various youth organizations such as the Boy Scouts of America and The Girls Scouts of America. Mary Jo has also directed summer youth camps for ten years.

© 1995 **Edupress** • P.O. Box 883 • Dana Point, CA 92629

ISBN 1-56472-066-7

TABLE OF CONTENTS

LITERATURE LIST

• **The Bear on the Moon**
by Joanne Ryder;
Morrow LB 1991. (K-3)
A story about the creation of the Arctic Circle involves a white bear who climbs the northern lights to visit the moon.

• **Berry Woman's Children**
by Dale De Armond;
Greenwillow 1985. (K-3)
Eskimo animal stories combine myth, folklore and daily life.

• **The Seal Oil Lamp**
by Dale De Armond;
Little 1988. (1-4)
According to Eskimo law, a blind child cannot be allowed to live if he cannot grow up to take care of himself.

• **Eskimo Boy: Life in an Inupiag Eskimo Village**
by Russ Kendall;
Scholastic 1991. (2-4)
A photo essay focusing on 7-year-old Norman Kokeok, who lives on the remote Alaskan island of Shishmaref.

• **Polar Bear Cubs**
By Downs Matthews;
Simon & Schuster 1989. (2-5)
A factual account of the life of polar bears in their cold climate.

• **Houses of Snow, Skin and Bones**
by Bonnie Shemie;
Tundra 1989. (3-6)
Covers a variety of dwellings used by people of the extreme north.

• **Arctic Memories**
by Normee Ekoomiak;
Henry Holt 1990. (3-5)
Memories of in Inuit artist who was raised in the James Bay area of arctic Quebec.

• **The Secret of the Seal**
by Deborah Davis;
Crown 1989. (3-5)
Kyo, a young Eskimo boy, must save the seal pup he has befriended.

• **The Falcon Bow: An Arctic Legend**
by James Houston;
Macmillan 1986. (4-6)
Kungo sets out to help the starving Inuits.

• **Destimation: Antarctica**
by Robert Swan;
Scholastic paper 1988. (3-7)
The story of Robert Scott, who reached the South Pole only to find it had already been "discovered" by Amundsen.

• **Don't Shoot**
by Roxane Chadwick;
Lerner LB 1979. (5-8)
A young Inuit boy must decide between saving a polar bear or a cruel hunter.

• **The Haunted Igloo**
by Bonnie Turner;
Houghton 1991. (4-7)
Ten-year-old Jean-Paul is sealed in a snow house with his Siberian husky pup in this story set in the 1930s.

• **Call of the Wild**
by Jack London;
Macmillan 1970. (6-8)
Enduring story of a dog in the Far North.

GLOBE PROJECT
HISTORICAL AID

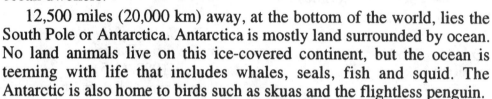

The North Pole, or Arctic Region, is at the top of the world. This frigid area is mostly ocean surrounded by land yet it supports many kinds of land animals such as polar bears and caribou, as well as a variety of ocean dwellers.

12,500 miles (20,000 km) away, at the bottom of the world, lies the South Pole or Antarctica. Antarctica is mostly land surrounded by ocean. No land animals live on this ice-covered continent, but the ocean is teeming with life that includes whales, seals, fish and squid. The Antarctic is also home to birds such as skuas and the flightless penguin.

PROJECT

Learn about the animal life of the Polar Regions by making a mural and placing the cut-outs in the correct region.

MATERIALS

• White butcher paper, about 24 inches (62 cm) square

• Glue

• Scissors

• Animal cut-outs

• Colored pencils or crayons

DIRECTIONS

1. Draw a large circle on the paper to represent the earth.

2. Draw in the continent of Antarctica and the edges of the countries that surround the Arctic Ocean forming the Arctic Region.

3. Color and cut out the animals. Glue them in place in the correct polar region.

Answer Key:

Arctic: Harp seal, caribou, polar bear, snowy owl, musk ox, walrus, beluga whale, arctic fox

Antarctic: Antarctic cod, Weddell seal, Leopard seal, skua, penguin, squid, blue whale

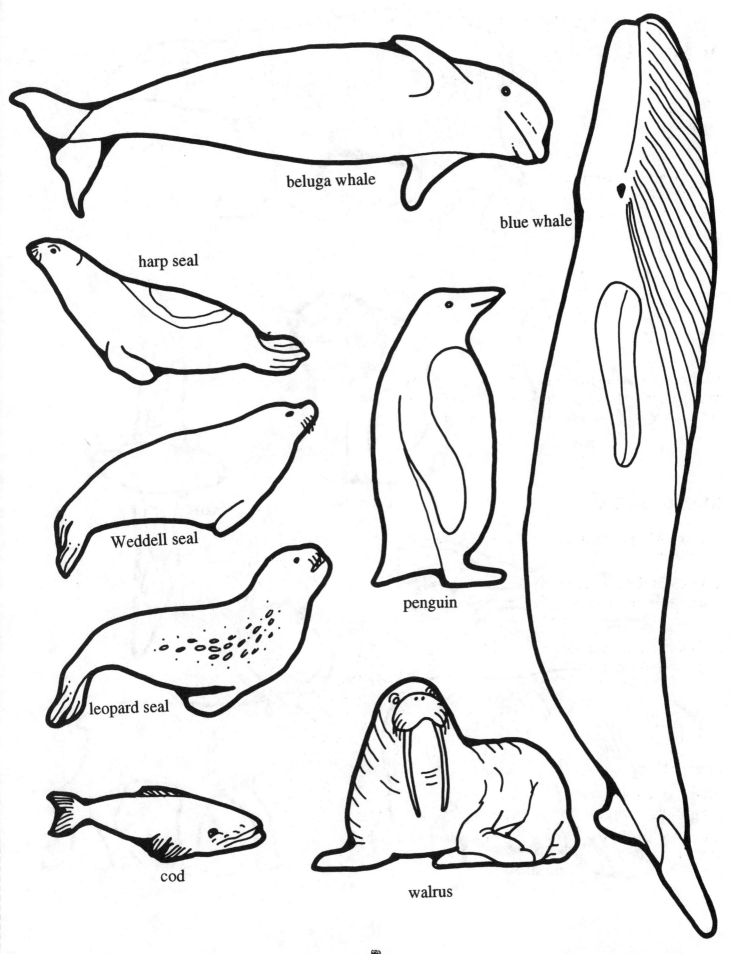

beluga whale

blue whale

harp seal

Weddell seal

leopard seal

penguin

cod

walrus

polar bear

snowy owl

arctic fox

skua

squid

musk ox

caribou

AURORA POLARIS
HISTORICAL AID

The *aurora polaris,* or polar light, is the name given to both the northern light (*aurora borealis*) and the southern light (*aurora austrialis*). These beautiful lights appear in the sky as dancing columns of different colors that assume an endless variety of forms including arches, streamers, bands, fans and—most often—waving curtains of light.

The light is made by electric storms 50 to 600 miles (80 to 930 km) above the earth, similar to the way light is made in a neon tube. This "high lightning" is different from the usual kind of lightning as there is rarely any noise at all, even during the fiercest storm.

PROJECT

Have fun with flashlights and simulate an aurora polaris in a darkened classroom.

MATERIALS

- Flashlights
- Red, green, yellow and blue cellophane
- Scissors
- Rubber bands

DIRECTIONS

1. Have students bring flashlights from home. Cut cellophane into circles and attach to the flashlights with rubber bands.

2. Darken the classroom and make an *aurora polaris* light show! After a little practice, call out the names of some shapes and work together to recreate them on the ceiling. Try arches, waving curtains, a glow, streamers and fans.

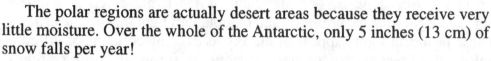

WHITEOUT

HISTORICAL AID

The polar regions are actually desert areas because they receive very little moisture. Over the whole of the Antarctic, only 5 inches (13 cm) of snow falls per year!

Whiteout is a phenomenon that occurs in polar regions when sunlight reflects back and forth between snow and sky until the horizon disappears and nothing but white can be seen. When this occurs, it is almost impossible to distinguish between sky and land since there is no visible horizon.

PROJECT

Make a torn paper collage of a polar landscape to imagine what a whiteout would be like.

MATERIALS

- White construction paper
- Glue

DIRECTIONS

1. Tear pieces of white paper into strips to create cliffs, snowdrifts, igloos, etc.

2. Glue pieces to a larger sheet of white paper to create a polar landscape during whiteout conditions.

3. Imagine what it would be like to live in a world that was all white. What would be some of the dangers of whiteout to the early Inuit and the modern pilot? What would be some safety measures you would have to follow if you were to live or travel in a polar region?

MAGNETIC POLES

HISTORICAL AID

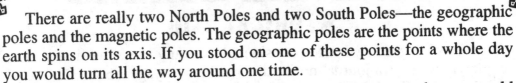

There are really two North Poles and two South Poles—the geographic poles and the magnetic poles. The geographic poles are the points where the earth spins on its axis. If you stood on one of these points for a whole day you would turn all the way around one time.

If you followed a compass needle pointing north far enough, you would come to a point where the compass needle would spin wildly round and round. You would be at the magnetic North Pole, hundreds of miles from the geographic pole. The same thing would happen traveling south!

PROJECT

Children will learn about the earth's magnetic field by using a drawing of the earth, iron filings and a magnet to create a "picture" of the earth's magnetic field.

MATERIALS

• Paper

• Drawing compass or plate to trace around

• Crayons or colored pencils

• Ruler

• Small bar magnet

• Iron filings

DIRECTIONS

1. Explain why the earth has a magnetic field. As the earth rotates, the crust spins at a faster rate than the heavy inner core. Both the core and the crust contain many metallic rocks. As these two metallic layers pass each other, they create a magnetic field. It's as if the earth has a giant bar magnet in it!

2. Draw a picture of the earth making the diameter about about twice the length of the magnet. Using a ruler, draw a line down the center of the earth to represent the north-south axis.

3. Put the magnet under the paper, tilted slightly away from the geographic North. The earth's magnetic field is tilted 11 degrees away from the axis on which the earth spins!

4. Sprinkle the iron filings evenly over the paper and tap it gently. The filings will arrange themselves along the lines of magnetic force.

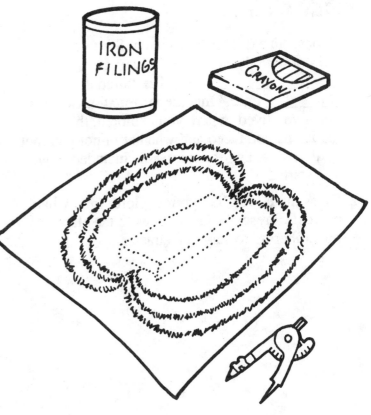

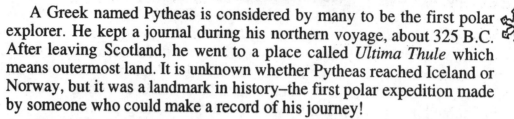

POLAR EXPLORERS
HISTORICAL AID

A Greek named Pytheas is considered by many to be the first polar explorer. He kept a journal during his northern voyage, about 325 B.C. After leaving Scotland, he went to a place called *Ultima Thule* which means outermost land. It is unknown whether Pytheas reached Iceland or Norway, but it was a landmark in history—the first polar expedition made by someone who could make a record of his journey!

Since then, many brave explorers have braved incredible hardships in their exploration of the polar regions. Their stories are fascinating accounts of incredible adventures by men of courage and stamina.

PROJECT

Learn about the Polar explorers by researching an explorer and presenting the findings to the class.

MATERIALS

- Paper or index cards
- Pen or pencil
- Encyclopedia
- Dress up clothes

DIRECTIONS

1. Choose an explorer to research. Start your writing with the sentence, "My name is _____ and I explored the _____ Pole." Include information such as when you lived, where you explored, the hardships you faced and whether or not you met your goal. A list of explorers is included to get you started.

2. Dress up to look like your explorer (many had beards!). Present your findings to the class, remembering to stay in character.

POLAR EXPLORERS

Roald Amundsen (1872–1928) and his team were the first group of explorers to reach the South Pole on December 14, 1911. These skilled explorers used the same type of sled dogs used by the natives of the Arctic to help them reach their goal.

Amundsen was an author as well as lecturer, adventurer and explorer. In May 1926, Amundsen crossed the pole in a blimp! Amundsen died during a rescue mission.

Robert Edwin Peary (1856–1920) made several unsuccessful attempts to reach the North Pole in 1905–1906, coming to within 174 miles (280 km) of the pole on one trip! He did not give up, and on July 17, 1908 he led another expedition to the pole. This time he was successful and on April 7, 1909, Peary, his African–American assistant, Matt Henson, and four Inuit guides reached their goal!

Sir James Clark Ross (1800–1862) was a rear admiral in the British Navy. He was the first explorer to penetrate the ice pack around Antarctica in 1841 and discover the ice shelf we call Ross Ice Shelf. It is on this ice shelf that most 20th century explorers have made their base camps. During Sir Ross' survey, he discovered twin volcanoes that he named after his ships, the "Erebus" and "Terror". His ships were almost sunk when they collided amid icebergs!

Sir John Franklin (1786–1847) and his 128 crew members perished when their ship lay trapped for *two years* in a mass of ice that jammed the Victoria Channel. Lady Franklin sent four ships to look for her husband. She gave the captains a map drawn after a seance with the spirit of a four year old girl who had recently died in Ireland. The ships arrived too late but the map proved accurate.

Other teams of explorers did not survive the brutal Antarctic weather. In a race with Amundsen to the pole, **Robert Falcon Scott** depended on ponies to haul gear. The ponies died, and although Scott did make it to the pole, he arrived after Amundsen. Scott and his team perished on the return trip. Scott's diaries were later published as *Scott's Last Expedition* and tell stories of bravery and adventure.

Richard Evelyn Byrd (1988–1957) made several expeditions to the Antarctic. With Floyd Bennet as co-pilot, he made the first flight over the North Pole in 1926. Byrd was awarded the Medal of Honor for this achievement. During the first polar expedition in 1928–1930, Byrd was able to establish a base called *Little America* on the Bay of Whales. He wrote many books about his adventures.

NIGHT SKIES

HISTORICAL AID

The name *Arctic* comes from the the Greek word *arctos,* or bear, because that is the name the Greeks gave the constellation over the North Pole. This group of stars, called Little Bear, includes Polaris, the North Star. Because of the earth's rotation, the entire sky seems to revolve around this star, located 780 light years away. Polaris is the first star in the handle of the Little Dipper. The word *Antarctica* means "opposite the bear" which makes sense when you consider that the continent of Antarctica is located at the opposite, or southern side of the earth.

PROJECT

Learn about the constellation called Little Bear (Ursa Minor) by making a stellar model.

MATERIALS

- Cardboard oatmeal box
- Straight pin
- Flashlight
- Tape
- Dark room

DIRECTIONS

1. Make a copy of the constellation pattern.

2. Tape the pattern to the bottom of the box. Use the pin to make the holes in the box.

3. Turn on the flashlight and place the box over the top so the light shines out through the holes. Go into a dark room and you will be able to see the constellation Little Bear reflecting out through the holes.

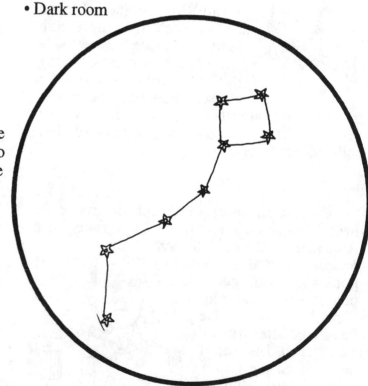

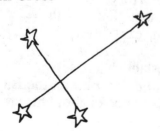

Southern Cross

(Ursa Minor) Little Bear

SEALS
HISTORICAL AID

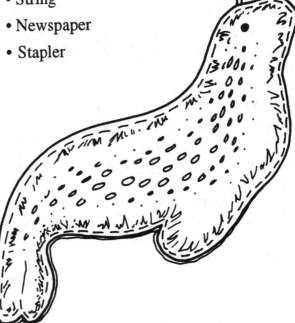

Seals are *pinnipeds,* or fin–footed mammals. There are three families of seals. Eared seals include sea lions and fur seals. Like walruses, the second family of seals, eared seals have back flippers that can be used for "walking" on ice. Antarctic seals belong to the third group of seals called earless, or true seals. Their flippers are bent backward for better swimming so they are very awkward on land.

Seals cannot breathe under water, so they claw "chimneys" through the ice. These holes also allow the seals to pop up onto the ice. Polar bears and hunters sometimes are waiting for the seals at these breathing holes.

Even though they live in frigid water, seals keep warm because they are protected by thick layers of fat and oily fur coats.

PROJECT

Learn about the different varieties of polar seals.

DIRECTIONS

1. There are 31 different species of seals. Choose one to research. Be able to tell the name of your seal and where it lives. Take a large piece of paper about 18 inches x 32 inches (50 cm x 83 cm). Fold in half. Trace a large outline (about 18 inches /50 cm tall) of your seal onto one side of the paper.

2. Cut out around the outline so you have two seal patterns. Paint the seal, making one side the front of your seal and the other side the back.

3. When the paint is dry, lightly stuff the seal with newspaper and staple closed. Hang from the ceiling with string. Pretend you are in the ocean and the ceiling is a layer of ice. Imagine that your seal is swimming up to the surface to find a breathing hole.

MATERIALS

- Encyclopedia
- Pencil
- Large sheets of white paper
- Tempera paint
- Paint brushes
- Scissors
- String
- Newspaper
- Stapler

THE ARCTIC
HISTORICAL AID

The Arctic is is the land and sea at the top of the world. It covers a huge area that includes the northernmost parts of Canada, the United States, Greenland, Iceland, Russia, Finland and Norway.

An open, grassy plain called the *tundra* covers much of the Arctic's land area. Creeping shrubs, grasses, mosses and herbs thrive in the harsh climate. Because of these hardy grasses, the tundra is sometimes called the "arctic prairie". Most of this frigid land is north of the timber line where trees cannot grow.

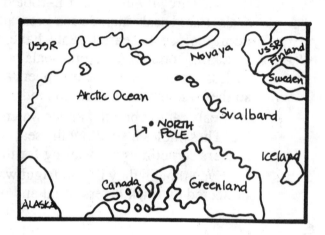

The Arctic is one of the coldest places on the earth. Winter is long and cold and summer is short and cool! Much of the Arctic Ocean's surface water is frozen in layers of sea ice. Most of the land is consists of permanently frozen ground or *permafrost*. Winter temperatures in the Arctic can reach -80°F (-65°C). During winter, which lasts nearly eight months, the temperature remains below zero for months.

Surprisingly, it does not snow much in the Arctic. Precipitation is so low that the region can be considered a desert!

During the short spring and summer, parts of the Arctic change from sea ice to open ocean. As temperatures reach 70°F (21°C) the snow disappears from large areas of the tundra. Mosses and lichen begin to grow, flowers bloom, insects and birds fill the sky and herds of caribou move northward. The Arctic is often called the Land of the Midnight Sun because during the Arctic summer, the sun never sets.

THE ARCTIC
HISTORICAL AID

The Arctic Ocean is the home of a variety of animal life including fish, seals, walrus, and whales. Coastal waters are rich in such fish as cod, flatfish, halibut, salmon and trout.

Land animals include lemmings, rabbits, squirrels, musk oxen, caribou, weasels, wolves, foxes and polar bears.

Almost one hundred varieties of birds nest on the tundra each summer. The guillemot and little auk nest by the thousands along cliffs. Ravens, snow buntings and gulls have been spotted in very remote regions. Gulls, loons, puffins and ptarmigan range far to the north. Perhaps the most well known of the Arctic birds is the Snowy Owl, a beautiful bird that was considered sacred by the early inhabitants of the Arctic.

Bees, wasps, flies, butterflies and grasshoppers can be found wherever there is vegetation growing.

People have lived in the Arctic for thousands of years. Long before Europeans reached the Arctic, much of the region had a scattered population. These people were of many ethnic groups, and spoke a variety of languages, but all had originated in Asia. Three main ethnic groups inhabited the Arctic areas of North America. The Aleut mostly occupied the region of the Bering Sea. Tribes of Native Americans inhabited the grasslands. The Inuit mostly lived in northern Alaska, Canada and coastal Greenland.

The name *Eskimo* comes from the word *Eskimantsic* which means "Eaters of Raw Meat". Inhabitants of the grasslands gave this name to the early inhabitants of the Arctic regions. The name these people gave themselves, however was *Inuit,* which simply means "People". These hardy nomads lived in a land covered with snow for most of the year. They hunted along the frozen shores and across the plains, depended on the caribou for survival and learned to adapt to the cold, harsh environment.

Inuit life changed dramatically after the 1920's. Today's Inuit families respect and admire their strong and brave ancestors, but live a modern lifestyle.

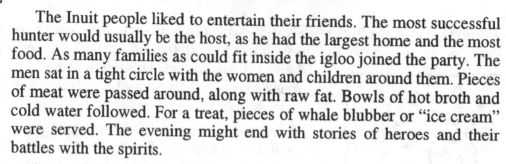

FEAST
HISTORICAL AID

The Inuit people liked to entertain their friends. The most successful hunter would usually be the host, as he had the largest home and the most food. As many families as could fit inside the igloo joined the party. The men sat in a tight circle with the women and children around them. Pieces of meat were passed around, along with raw fat. Bowls of hot broth and cold water followed. For a treat, pieces of whale blubber or "ice cream" were served. The evening might end with stories of heroes and their battles with the spirits.

PROJECT

Have a classroom feast serving recipes based on the foods served at an Inuit gathering. As the foods are served, be sure to explain what the actual ingredients would be.

MATERIALS

• See individual recipes and preparation ideas, following

• Bowl, plastic eating utensils

DIRECTIONS

1. Push the desks to one side of the classroom. With masking tape, make a large circle on the floor. This is the outline of the igloo. Lay down blankets to simulate the furs that were laid on the igloo floor.

2. About 4–5 hours before serving, make the stew in a slow cooker. Start heating the beef broth in another slow cooker about 1 hour before serving. The students can prepare the "ice cream".

3. At serving time, have the students sit in a circle inside the igloo. Pass around bowls of stew and strips of pemmican, followed by bowls of broth then bowls of water. For the treat serve bowls of "ice cream".

RECIPES

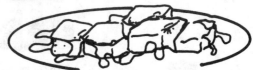

Meat such as caribou, which was eaten throughout the year, was boiled in stone vessels which took hours to heat in the subfreezing temperatures. Cooking used a great deal of seal oil that was the usual source of cooking fuel so the Inuit usually ate their meat raw or just barely warm. Every edible part of the animal was used in stew or soup or simply eaten raw. In the summer, greens and berries were added to the Inuit diet.

Caribou Stew

This stew is cooked for a far longer time than it would be in an authentic recipe.

Ingredients
2 pounds (4.4 Kg) stewing beef, cubed
2 cups (500 ml) beef broth

Place meat and beef broth into a slow cooker. Cover and cook on High setting for 4–5 hours.

Pemmican

This version substitutes peanut butter for fat, raisins for berries, adds nuts and honey and substitutes beef for caribou meat!

Ingredients:
Two 2½-ounce packages thinly sliced, pressed cooked beef.

2½ cups (625 ml) raisins

1½ cups (375 ml) chopped nuts

2 T (30 ml) honey

2 T (30 ml) peanut butter

Previous day: Separate meat slices on a cookie sheet. Place in a warm oven propping the door open a crack. Allow to dry about 8 hours.

Making the pemmican: Crush the dried meat. Mix in a bowl with raisins and nuts. Heat the honey and peanut butter until melted. Blend honey mixture into dry ingredients. Shape into flat patties.

Leftover meat and fish were dried and stored to be eaten when fresh meat was scarce. Dried meat was also used to make *pemmican* for hunters to carry on long expeditions. Inuit women made pemmican from crushed dried meat and berries kneaded together with fat and shaped into patties. This nutritious food could be stored for years.

Ice Cream

Inuit women whipped berries with bits of caribou fat, seal oil and snow to make ice cream. This recipe is not authentic.

Ingredients
1 bag frozen blueberries
Whipped topping

Defrost the blueberries almost all the way and mix with whipped topping.

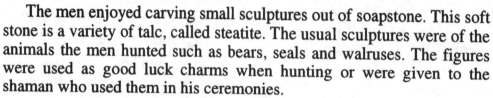

CARVINGS
HISTORICAL AID

During the long winter it is almost always dark. Inside the igloo, the Inuit families would work and play. Women sewed the skins together that would be used for the tent the family would live in during the summer.

The men enjoyed carving small sculptures out of soapstone. This soft stone is a variety of talc, called steatite. The usual sculptures were of the animals the men hunted such as bears, seals and walruses. The figures were used as good luck charms when hunting or were given to the shaman who used them in his ceremonies.

PROJECT

Design and carve an animal out of soap.

DIRECTIONS

1. Using a pencil, trace the design of the animal you wish to carve onto the soap. A bear or whale are good choices.

2. Carve out the figure with the knife, continuing to cut away a little at a time to make the figure look three-dimensional.

3. Use the toothpick to add details such as the eyes, fur, teeth and claws.

MATERIALS

• Large bar of soft soap, such as Dove

• Pencil

• Butter knife

• Toothpicks

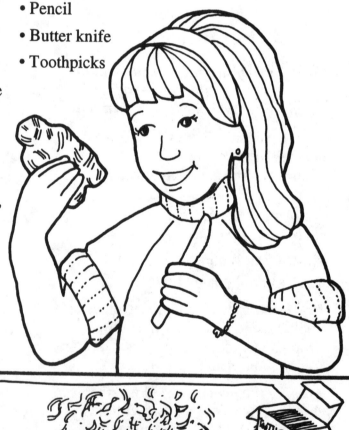

GAMES
HISTORICAL AID

Children's toys were made from natural objects such as bone or ivory, animal skins and fur and sometimes wood. Balls were often made of sealskin stuffed with moss and decorated with fringed strips of hide.

The Blanket Toss Game is a fun game that is among the many games played by both Inuit children and adults. It was based on a strategy that hunters would use to look for Caribou. A circle of men would hold a circle of walrus hide with the lookout on it. When they pulled the hide tight, the man would be tossed high in the air and could look for the herds.

PROJECT

Plan a game time and learn about Eskimo games by using similar toys.

DIRECTIONS

1. Set up a center where children can go to play Inuit games. Assemble the materials at right and prepare the games according to the instructions included in the game pages, following. Show children how to play each game.

MATERIALS

Blanket Toss
- Towels
- Stuffed animals or rag dolls

String Game
- String

Holes and Pin
- Heavy corrugated cardboard
- Tape
- Unsharpened pencil

Dice Game
- Self-hardening clay
- Toothpick

High Kick Game
- Long pole or broom handle
- Heavy strapping tape
- Soccer size ball
- Piece of line about 4 feet (1.2 m) long

Push Up Game
- Paper plates
- Licorice sticks

Twirling Ball Game
- 2 old tennis balls
- Scissors
- Piece of ⅛-inch (.4 cm) string about 3 feet (1 m) long

TWIRLING BALLS

1. Cut a hole in each end of two tennis balls. Cut two lengths of string, one about four inches (11 cm) longer than the other. Pass string through each ball. Knot the end to keep the ball from pulling off. Tie the unknotted ends together.

2. The object is to get the balls moving in opposite circles. The trick is to keep your hand moving up and down rather than around.

PUSH UP

1. Place a stick of licorice on a paper plate and pretend it is a stick lying on the icy ground. Do a push up and try to pick up the "stick" in your mouth.

STRING GAME

1. Cut a length of string about 36 inches (1 m) long. Tie at the ends to form a loop. Play a game of Cat's Cradle—it's very similar to the string game played by Inuit boys. Some boys know over two hundred different shapes to make with string. The shape of a kayak will take 22 different steps!

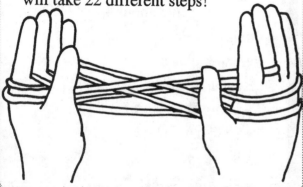

FUNNY FACES

1. Everyone gets a chance to make a funny face! The audience gets to vote on the one they think is the funniest.

HOLES AND PIN

1. Cut a cardboard rectangle 4 inches x 6 inches (10 cm x 16 cm). Trace and cut out three quarter-size circles from the cardboard.

2. Cut a piece of string 36 inches (1 m) long. Use tape to secure one end to the pencil. Tie the other end through one of the holes cut in the cardboard.

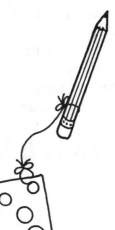

3. To play, hold the pencil or "pin" with the point up. Toss the cardboard into the air. Try to catch it on the pencil.

DICE

1. Shape salt dough clay (page 38) into 15 duck shapes about 1 inch (2.54 cm) each. Allow to dry in a 200° F (93° C) oven.

2. Spread a towel to simulate a game board. Two players sit on opposite sides. One player holds all the ducks and tosses them gently onto the towel. Each player gets to pick up the ducks that are facing his or her way. The next player picks up the remaining pieces and tosses them again. Play continues until all the pieces are picked up. The winner is the player with the most pieces.

BLANKET TOSS

1. Place a stuffed animal in the center of a sheet or blanket. One person holds each edge. Toss the stuffed animal into the air and try to catch it before it lands. You can also play in teams and toss the animal from blanket to blanket.

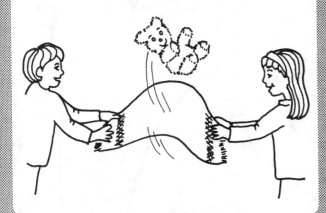

HIGH KICK

1. Use strapping tape to attach a 3 foot (1 m) length of rope to a soccer-size ball . Tie the other end of the rope to a long pole or broom handle.

2. To play the game, have one player hold the pole with the ball about a foot from the ground. Players take turns kicking the ball. Raise the pole higher and higher until only one person can kick the ball.

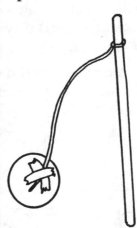

ICE FISHING

HISTORICAL AID

The caribou, which was the mainstay of the Inuit diet, migrated South for the long, hard Arctic winter. Winter storms made hunting seal and walrus very difficult. Families had food stored for the winter, but starvation was a constant fear. The entire family would go fishing for *char*, a kind of trout. After breaking a hole in the ice with a long pole, a fisherman would scoop out the broken ice with a large spoonlike shovel. The round frame of the scoop was made from bent bone, laced with whalebone and had a a long sturdy handle attached. Children had their own miniature scoops for helping to clear away the ice and just for play!

PROJECT

Inuit children were given miniature ice scoops to play with. Students can imagine they are Inuit children as they play a relay race game with a pretend ice scoop.

MATERIALS

• 4 buckets

• Ice cubes

• New, unused kitty litter scoops, OR slotted spoons

DIRECTIONS

1. Fill two buckets with cold water and several ice cubes. Place the other two buckets a distance away.

2. Form two teams. At the start signal, the first player runs to the bucket with the ice, scoops up an ice cube and runs to drop it in the other bucket. Then he runs back to the next player on his team and passes her the scoop.

3. Play continues until one team has scooped out all their ice and moved it to the second bucket.

22

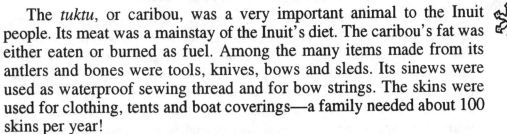

CARIBOU
HISTORICAL AID

The *tuktu*, or caribou, was a very important animal to the Inuit people. Its meat was a mainstay of the Inuit's diet. The caribou's fat was either eaten or burned as fuel. Among the many items made from its antlers and bones were tools, knives, bows and sleds. Its sinews were used as waterproof sewing thread and for bow strings. The skins were used for clothing, tents and boat coverings—a family needed about 100 skins per year!

When the Inuit hunted caribou, they built *inuksuk,* which were stone piles that looked like men. The caribou ran away from the rock statues toward the real hunters who were waiting for them.

PROJECT

Work as a cooperative group using cardboard boxes of various sizes to build a *inuksuk*.

MATERIALS

- Several boxes of various sizes
- Masking tape
- Grey paint
- Brushes
- Newspaper

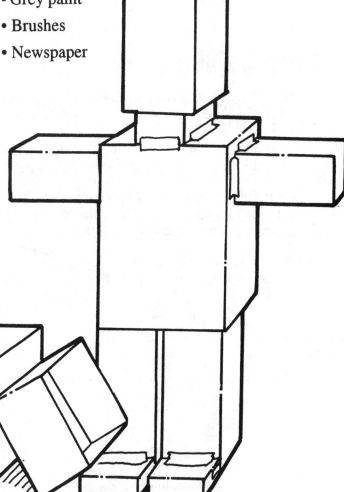

DIRECTIONS

1. Have the students bring in boxes of various sizes from home. While working with the boxes, the students can imagine that these are rocks different hunters found and brought together.

2. Have them arrange the boxes to create a sculpture of a man, taping the boxes together securely.

3. After spreading out newspaper to protect the area, the students can paint their *inuksuk* grey. Using a paintbrush dipped in black paint, students can gently flick black paint onto their "rocks" to give them a granite look.

UMIAKS

HISTORICAL AID

Walrus and whale hunting was often done from a boat called an *umiak.* A typical *umiak* was about five feet (1.6 m) wide and 30 feet (9 m) long, and made from a wooden or bone frame covered with skins. It had a flat bottom and high sides. This boat was very useful as it could carry heavy loads and yet was light enough to be carried by two men. Hunting crews in *umiaks* would surround a whale or walrus and attack it with harpoons. This was very dangerous as a wounded animal could could easily overturn the *umiaks* when it thrashed about in the water. A hunter who fell into the water did not often survive.

PROJECT

Learn about the construction of an *umiak* by building a model.

MATERIALS

• Pattern on facing page
• Lightweight cardboard
• Scissors
• Masking tape

DIRECTIONS

1. Cut the pattern from lightweight cardboard such as tagboard or a cereal box.

2. Fold up the cardboard along the dotted lines, bend in the tabs and fasten with masking tape.

3. Cut pieces of masking tape and cover the interior and exterior of the *umiak* with tape, pressing down the edges carefully.

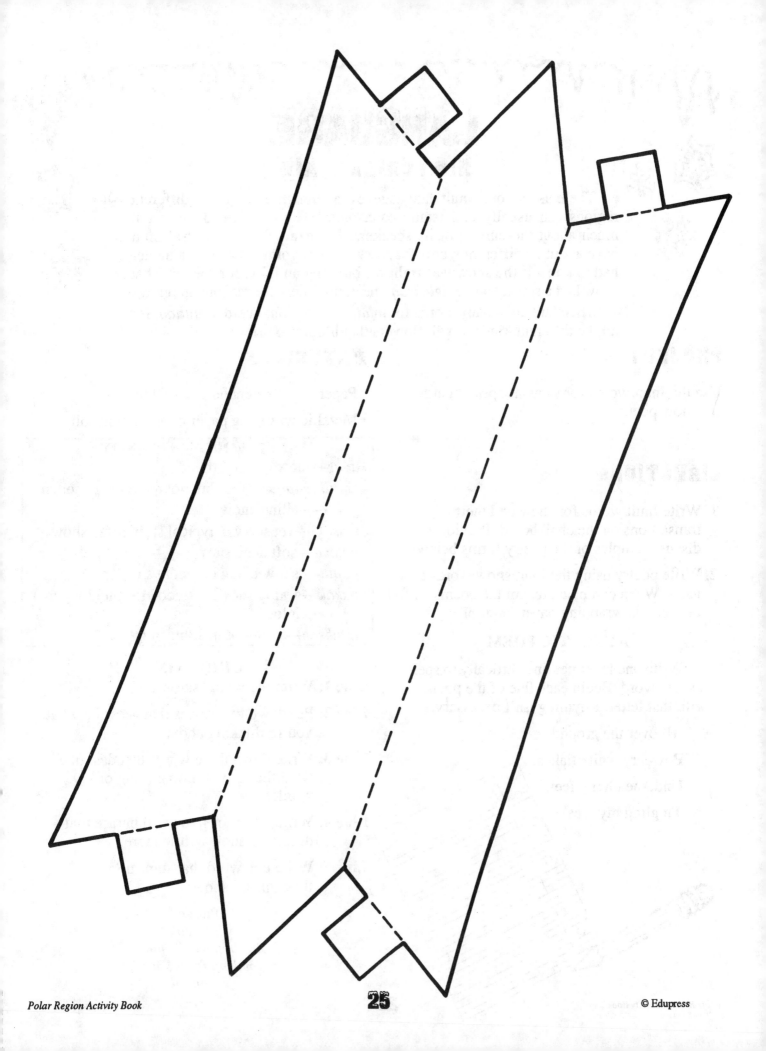

LANGUAGE
HISTORICAL AID

There is no one Inuit language even though Inuit from different regions can usually understand each other. The different dialects tell much about the culture of its speakers. For example, the Central Inuit have about 70 different words for *snow*. Before going on a hunt, a hunter had to know if the snow was right for building an igloo for shelter. That snow had a special name, *igluksaq*, meaning "snow for making an igloo".

There are also many words for *mud*, but only one word, *nauttiaq*, for all the different kinds of wildflowers that bloom so briefly.

PROJECT

Use the Inuit words for snow as springboards for snow poetry.

MATERIALS

- Paper
- Pencils
- Glue
- Metallic wrapping paper or aluminum foil

DIRECTIONS

1. Write Inuit words for snow and their translations on the chalkboard. Provide and discuss samples of the poetry forms below.

2. Write poetry using the Inuit snow words as a basis. When complete, mount the poems on foil or metallic wrapping paper for display.

ACROSTIC POEM

Write one letter per line vertically to spell a snow word. Begin each line of the poem with that letter. Rhyming isn't necessary.

All over the ground.

Powdery white flakes.

Underneath my feet.

Tingling my toes.

INUIT WORDS FOR SNOW
aput—snow on the ground
aquilluqqaqa—firm, but not quite firm enough
ganik—falling snow
masak—wet snow, a typical springtime snow
mauya—soft deep snow
piqtuq—snow being blown in a blizzard
pukak—grainy snow, not good for building an igloo
igluksaq—snow for making an igloo

CINQUAIN

Line 1: Write the word "snow".

Line 2: Put down two words that describe what you're thinking about.

Line 3: Write down three words that describe what the snow is doing (–ing or –ly words).

Line 4: Write a four or five word phrase that describes snow a little more.

Line 5: Write one word that sums up your thoughts on snow.

Piqtuq
white, cold
blowing, windy, harsh
making faces sting
beautiful

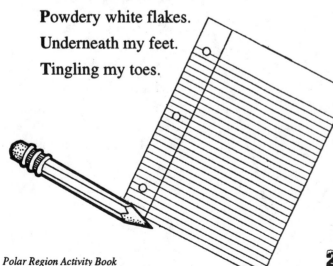

CELEBRATION

HISTORICAL AID

Among the celebrations enjoyed by different Inuit groups is *Petugta*, a gift–giving festival. At the time of the festival, men would hang miniature replicas of things they wanted such as mittens made from skins, grass socks or birdskin caps, on sticks. The women had made these things without knowing who would receive their gift. When it came time to match the receiver of the gift with its maker, everyone had a laugh at some of the strange match–ups.

PROJECT

Play a match–up game based on the Inuit *Petugtaq* celebration in your classroom using pictures of gifts cut from a catalog.

MATERIALS

- Gift catalogs
- Scissors
- Craft sticks or paint stirrers
- Paper plates
- Glue

DIRECTIONS

1. Make two sets of "gifts" by cutting pictures of items from catalogs and gluing them to paper plates.

2. Glue one set of pictures to craft sticks or paint stirrers.

3. Play a classroom game of concentration. Each student receives a paper plate. The boys may use the plates on sticks and pretend they are Inuit men who have hung the replica of their wished-for gift on a stick. Girls may use the paper plates without sticks and pretend they have made the gift they are about to give away. Students take turns guessing which players have matching cards.

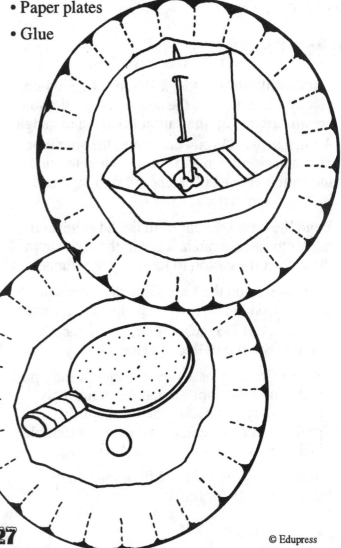

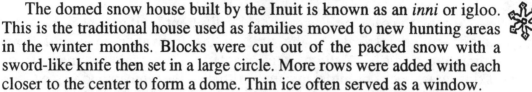

IGLOO

HISTORICAL AID

The domed snow house built by the Inuit is known as an *inni* or igloo. This is the traditional house used as families moved to new hunting areas in the winter months. Blocks were cut out of the packed snow with a sword-like knife then set in a large circle. More rows were added with each closer to the center to form a dome. Thin ice often served as a window.

Loose snow was packed into the gaps between the blocks and a tunnel was built as an entry way either underground or on the side of the igloo away from the wind. It only takes an hour or two to build an igloo!

PROJECT

Build a model of an Inuit igloo.

MATERIALS

- Large sour cream container
- Piece of white tagboard, 6 x 6 inches (16 x 16 cm) for base
- Scissors
- Tape
- Glue
- Premixed spackling compound
- Small bit of modeling clay
- Brown felt or construction paper
- Crayons

DIRECTIONS

1. Cut the meat tray into 1 x 1½-inch (2.5 x 4 cm) pieces. Carefully cut the bottom out of the sour cream carton. Cut the carton lid into a rectangle 4 x 1½ inches (11 x 4 cm). Turn the sour cream carton upside down and cut an arch in the side of the carton about 11/2 inches (4 cm) high and 1 inch (2.5 cm) across.

2. Bend the rectangle cut from the lid in several places to form an arch. Tape in the arch cut in the side of the carton to form an entry tunnel.

4. Set the igloo on the base. Glue the foam squares to the carton in two rows. Cut eight long, narrow pieces (about 1½ inches/4 cm by x 1 inch/2.5 cm) for the entry. Glue in place. Let dry.

5. Using a fingertip or a popsicle stick, gently push spackle into the gaps around the foam. This dries quickly and makes the igloo sturdy. Spackle can be spread on the base to resemble drifting snow.

6. Furnish the igloo. Use the floor plan on the following page for ideas.

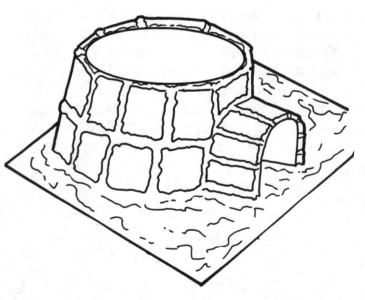

IGLOO CROSS SECTION

IGLERK   One third of the inside of the floor of an igloo was taken up by a raised platform of snow called the "iglerk". This served as a table or couch by day and a bed by night. Caribou hides and sealskins were used as blankets and to cover the walls if the family would be staying in the igloo for awhile.

Use pieces of foam to build up a platform inside the igloo, Cut pieces of felt or brown paper to look like hides and cover the platform.

FOOD SUPPLY   The family's food supply of frozen fish and seals is stacked along the wall.

Cut out and color fish from tagboard scraps to lay along the wall of the igloo.

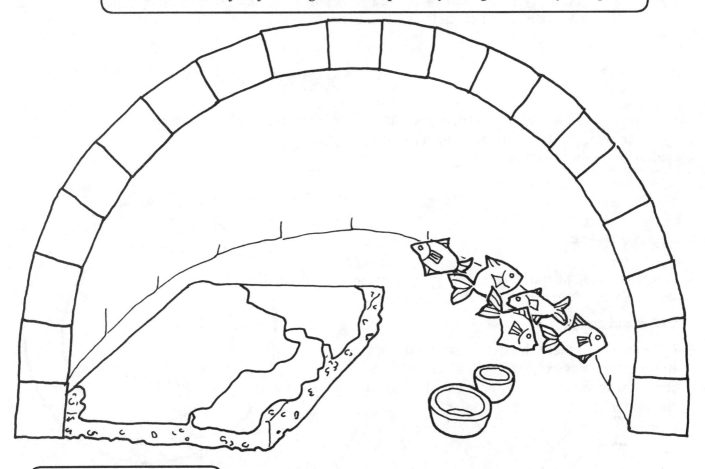

LAMP & BOWL   An igloo was heated and lit by a lamp that used a moss wick and burned blubber as fuel. This lamp was a bowl carved from soapstone and often was set on a stand of three wooden legs. The bowls and cooking utensils used by the Inuit people were also carved from soapstone.

Use clay to make two bowls—one slightly larger than the other. Use the smaller as an eating dish and the larger as a lamp. When the clay hardens put the bowls on the floor.

SONG AND DANCE

HISTORICAL AID

Ancient legends, hunting adventures, stories of the spirits and everyday life were the subjects of Inuit song and dance. Singing was such a big part of Inuit daily life that some arguments were settled with a song contest! Whoever composed the funniest song that best insulted his rival would be the winner!

Dancing was done to the beat of drums made of skins stretched over a wooden hoop. There were ceremonial dances, but dancing was also done just for fun. At a celebration, the men and women would bend their knees and sway to the beat of the drum. A singer would share his song, and everyone would chant the refrain between verses.

PROJECT

Make a replica of the small wooden masks that the women wore on their first two fingers when they danced in special ceremonies.

MATERIALS

- White paper plates or tagboard
- Scissors
- Colored pencils or crayons

DIRECTIONS

1. Copy the mask pattern onto tagboard or a paper plate.

2. Color and cut out.

3. Tell in song or dance the story of an imaginary hunting trip. For example, act out a trip across the snow to the hunting ground and the wait at the seal's hole in the ice.

Pattern

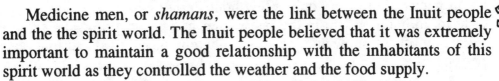

SHAMAN
HISTORICAL AID

Medicine men, or *shamans*, were the link between the Inuit people and the the spirit world. The Inuit people believed that it was extremely important to maintain a good relationship with the inhabitants of this spirit world as they controlled the weather and the food supply.

A shaman was the most powerful member of a band and was responsible for preventing and healing sickness and interpreting messages from the spirit world. To communicate with the spirits, a shaman would go into a trance and send his spirit great distances.

PROJECT

Make a pouch similar to one a Shaman might have used to used to carry his amulets or charms.

MATERIALS

• Brown felt or fabric

• Hole punch

• Long brown shoelace or strips of brown fabric about 24 inches (62 cm) long

• Scissors

DIRECTIONS

1. Cut a circle of felt about 8 inches (22 cm) in diameter. Use the hole punch to make holes around the outside of the circle about 1 inch (2.5 cm) apart.

2. Weave the shoelace or fabric strip through the holes. Tie the end of the strips together into a knot.

3. Place a favorite object such as a pretty stone of marble or feather in the bag. Close the pouch and wear it around your neck if you wish.

SNOW GOGGLES
HISTORICAL AID

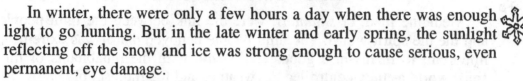

In winter, there were only a few hours a day when there was enough light to go hunting. But in the late winter and early spring, the sunlight reflecting off the snow and ice was strong enough to cause serious, even permanent, eye damage.

To solve this problem, the Inuits invented snow goggles which were made out of wood, antler or animal hooves. Small slits let the wearer see out, but let in very little light. Often the goggles were carved to resemble seals, and were not only functional, but beautiful as well.

PROJECT

Make snow goggles, an Inuit invention.

MATERIALS

- Egg carton
- Scissors
- Marking pens
- Hole punch
- String

DIRECTIONS

1. Use the pattern to cut snow goggles from the lid of an egg carton. Carefully cut two thin slits in the lid as shown. Using the hole punch, make two holes as shown.

2. Decorate the goggles with markers to look like carvings.

3. Tie string through the holes and pretend they are strips of leather used to tie on the goggles.

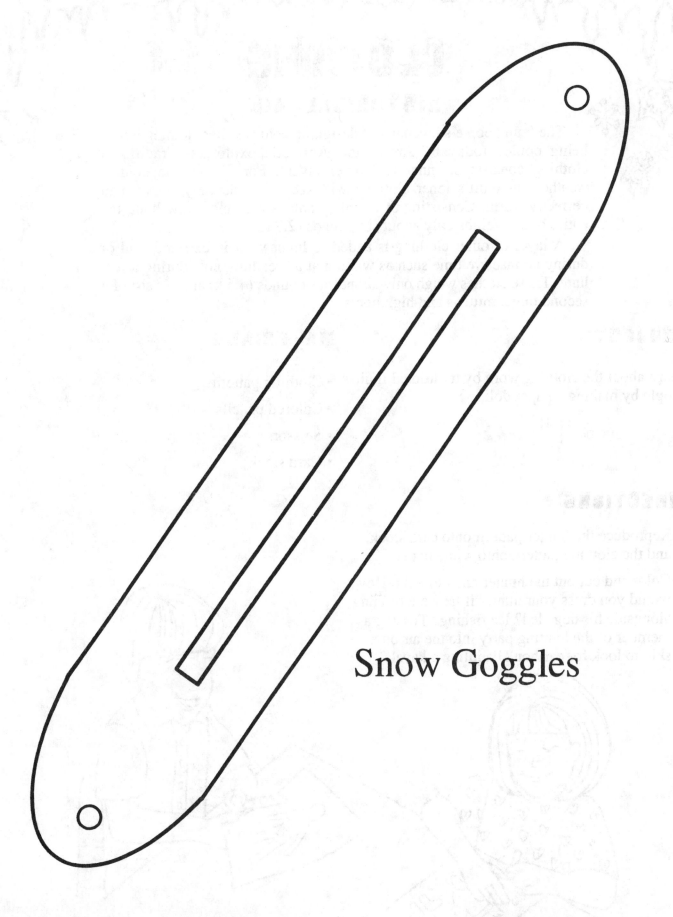

Snow Goggles

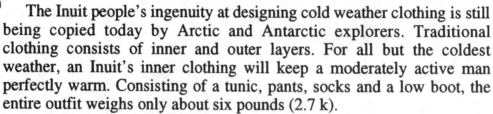

CLOTHING
HISTORICAL AID

The Inuit people's ingenuity at designing cold weather clothing is still being copied today by Arctic and Antarctic explorers. Traditional clothing consists of inner and outer layers. For all but the coldest weather, an Inuit's inner clothing will keep a moderately active man perfectly warm. Consisting of a tunic, pants, socks and a low boot, the entire outfit weighs only about six pounds (2.7 k).

A layer of outer clothing is added to inner wear in extreme cold or during an inactive time such as waiting at a breathing hole during a seal hunt. These clothes weigh only about four pounds (4.5 k) and consist of a second tunic, mittens and high boots.

PROJECT

Learn about the clothing worn by traditional Inuit people by making a paper doll.

MATERIALS

• Clothing pattern
• Colored pencils
• Scissors
• Card stock

DIRECTIONS

1. Reproduce the hunter pattern onto card stock, and the clothing pattern onto white paper.

2. Color and cut out the hunter and clothing. How would you dress your hunter if he were running alongside his dog sled? Ice fishing? Tossing a member of the hunting party into the air on a skin to look for caribou? Paddling a kayak?

INNER CLOTHING

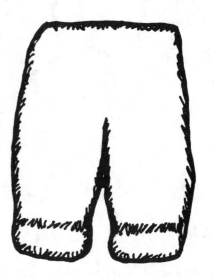

Pants are made from polar bear or caribou pelts and extend only just below the top of the boots. The pants are worn tucked into the boots.

The tunic is made from soft fur or bird skins, and has the hair or feathers inside to provide an air space in which the warm air from the body collects. The tunic is designed to keep body heat in—there are no button holes and the seams are tightly sewn.

A fur sock is usually worn, with the fur side inward. This sock is loose-fitting and is packed with fry grass. The grass is frequently changed to keep the feet dry. Sometimes a low boot that resembles a slipper is worn over the sock.

OUTER CLOTHING

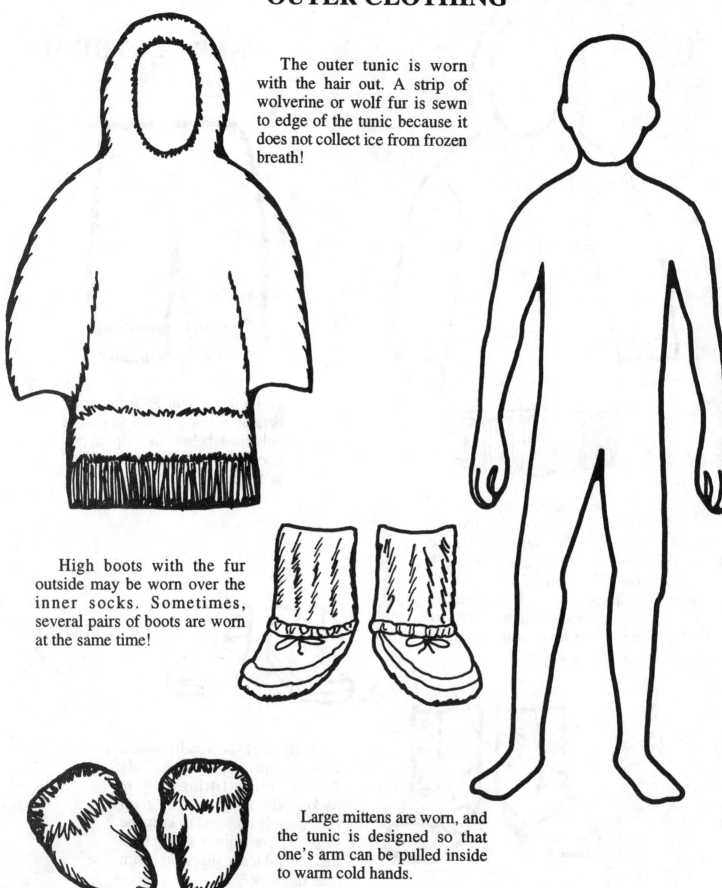

The outer tunic is worn with the hair out. A strip of wolverine or wolf fur is sewn to edge of the tunic because it does not collect ice from frozen breath!

High boots with the fur outside may be worn over the inner socks. Sometimes, several pairs of boots are worn at the same time!

Large mittens are worn, and the tunic is designed so that one's arm can be pulled inside to warm cold hands.

MASKS
HISTORICAL AID

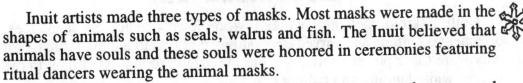

Inuit artists made three types of masks. Most masks were made in the shapes of animals such as seals, walrus and fish. The Inuit believed that animals have souls and these souls were honored in ceremonies featuring ritual dancers wearing the animal masks.

Some masks were used in plays. The medicine man, or shaman, used other masks in certain ceremonies. Masks were most often made of driftwood and enlarged with extended rims or feathers. The masks were usually painted white or blue with red highlights.

PROJECT

Design and make an Inuit ceremonial style mask.

DIRECTIONS

1. Make the clay, and pat into an oval about 12 inches (32 cm) long. Use the plastic fork to form the mouth. Poke holes in the clay to form eyes and nostrils. Poke holes around the outside to insert feathers after the mask has been painted. Let dry.

2. Paint the mask white. Outline the features with red or blue and glue the feathers into the holes.

MATERIALS

- Clay recipe, page 38
- Tempera paint
- Toothpicks
- Plastic forks
- Brushes
- Feathers
- Glue

AMULETS
HISTORICAL AID

Both Eskimo men and women wore jewelry such as necklaces, ornamental buttons and carved decorations that tied to a hunter's hat. Not only were these pieces decorative, but they also brought good luck to the wearer while hunting and fishing.

A necklace made from the teeth of seals, for example, was used as a magical charm to bring the wearer power over other sea mammals. To give him strength during a long hunting expedition, a hunter might attach a polar bear's nose to his clothing.

PROJECT

Make a necklace and a hat ornament in the style of the early Eskimos.

DIRECTIONS

Sea Mammal Necklace

1. **SALT DOUGH RECIPE** Combine salt and flour. Add just a little water until the dough feels like modeling clay.

2. Form the clay into teeth about ½ inch (1.3 cm) wide. You will need about 30-40 teeth. Use a toothpick to make a hole through the top of each tooth so they can be strung together.

3. Bake the teeth at 200°F (92°C) until hard, checking every 10 minutes.

4. String the teeth together to form a necklace.

Bone Hat Ornament

1. Have an adult make a hole in the top of the wooden ice cream spoon using the hammer and nail.

2. Using the marking pens, make a design on the spoon. Use a piece of string to simulate the sinew used to tie the ornament onto the hunter's hat.

MATERIALS

- 1 cup (250 ml) flour
- 1 cup (250 ml) salt
- Toothpick
- String
- Blunt needle
- Wooden ice cream spoons
- Marking pens
- Hammer and nail

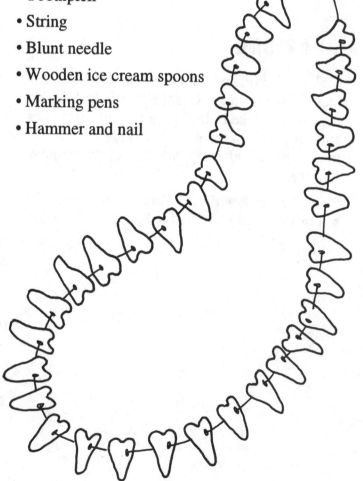

ENGRAVING

HISTORICAL AID

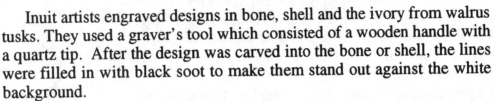

Inuit artists engraved designs in bone, shell and the ivory from walrus tusks. They used a graver's tool which consisted of a wooden handle with a quartz tip. After the design was carved into the bone or shell, the lines were filled in with black soot to make them stand out against the white background.

Many objects such as pipe stems, spoons, hat decorations and other tools were decorated in this manner. The designs often used pictograph to illustrate stories of daily life and hunting expeditions.

PROJECT

Learn about incising a design and about pictographs (a picturelike symbol representing an idea) by making an "ivory" engraving.

MATERIALS

- Foam meat trays
- Scissors
- Paper
- Pencil
- Black pen or permanent marker

DIRECTIONS

1. Cut the foam tray into a tusk-like shape.

2. Plan a design on paper that tells a story such as shooting a bow during a hunt, paddling a kayak or building an igloo. Use stick figures and simple designs.

3. Lightly trace the design in the foam using a sharp pencil. Then incise, or engrave, the design into the foam by pressing down on the pencil as you trace over the lines.

4. Trace over the lines one more time, this time using a black pen to give the appearance of soot rubbed into the design.

ABOUT THE ANTARCTIC

Antarctica is the fifth largest continent. It is surrounded by parts of three oceans: the Atlantic, Indian and Pacific Oceans. These frigid waters are also known as the Southern Ocean. Antarctica is mostly circular in shape with a long arm called the Antarctic Peninsula and two dents—the Ross and Weddell seas.

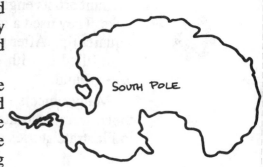

SOUTH POLE

More than 95% of Antarctica is covered with ice. This awesome ice cover is constantly moving. Great rivers of ice slowly inch toward the sea and form the ice shelves. Large flat-topped icebergs form as the edges of ice shelves and glaciers break, or calve off into the sea. Ice also extends over vast areas of the sea—the Ross Ice Shelf is a floating ice shelf that is large as the state of Texas!

Antarctica is the coldest continent. On August 24, 1960, the temperature dropped to −126°F (−88.3°C)! Heavy winds blow across the antarctic. Winds as high as 200 mph (320 km/hr) have been recorded in the interior.

Antarctica can be classified as a true desert; only about 2 inches (50 mm) of precipitation fall each year. Fierce blizzards are frequent, however, as the howling wind blows the existing snow.

The interior has almost continuous daylight during the summer and almost continuous darkness during the winter.

Very little vegetation exists in Antarctica. The few species of plants that do survive are mostly found in the rare ice–free areas on the Antarctic Peninsula. Most vegetation consists of mosses and lichens.

No land mammals live in the Antarctic, but the ocean is home to a wide variety of marine life including fish, squid and whales. Six species of seals and about twelve species of birds live in this southern polar region. The Antarctic ice is home to millions of penguins, the most typical being the Emperor and the Adelie.

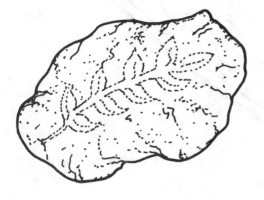

Much scientific research is happening in Antarctica in the areas of weather control, seismology, meteorology, and glaciology, among others. Fossils found by paleontologists help piece together the history of an ancient supercontinent called Gondwanaland. Geologists have found meteors and moon fragments and volcanologists study Antarctica's two volcanos. The discovery of the "ozone–hole" was made in 1985 by a British scientist studying weather.

SURVIVAL SKILLS
HISTORICAL AID

No climate on earth is more potentially dangerous to man than that of Antarctica. Temperatures there have been recorded as low as 126.9 °F below zero (−88.3°C)! Yet this icy continent forms a unique laboratory for all kinds of scientific investigation. Marine biologists, geologists, oceanographers and many other types of scientists live, work and study at research bases throughout Antarctica.

Unlike the early polar explorers, these present day scientific teams live and travel in relative comfort and safety. The *Polar Manual* was written by a doctor to keep naval personnel safe while they were stationed in a polar region. It included some ways to signal for help.

PROJECT

Play a game and learn some body signals used by polar survivors to signal a plane.

MATERIALS

- 2 flashlights
- Red and green cellophane
- 2 rubber bands

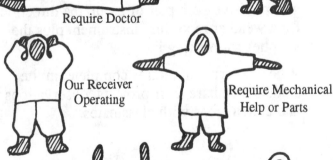

Use Drop Message

Require Doctor

DIRECTIONS

1. Use rubber bands to secure red cellophane over the top of one flashlight and green cellophane over the top of the other flashlight.

2. One player pretends to be a polar survivor and sends a message to the rescue plane using the following signals from the *Polar Manual*.

3. The pilot answers by flashing a red light for "not understood" or a green light for "O.K."

Our Receiver Operating

Require Mechanical Help or Parts

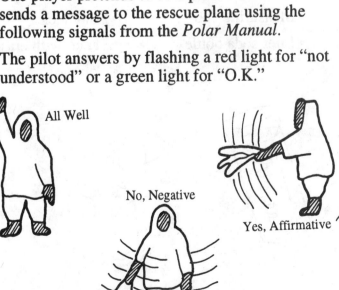

All Well

No, Negative

Yes, Affirmative

Pick Us Up Aircraft Abandoned

Can Proceed, or Wait

Don't Land Here

Land Here, Pointing Direction

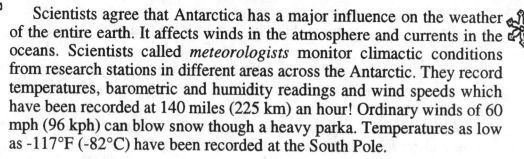

WEATHER STATION

HISTORICAL AID

Scientists agree that Antarctica has a major influence on the weather of the entire earth. It affects winds in the atmosphere and currents in the oceans. Scientists called *meteorologists* monitor climactic conditions from research stations in different areas across the Antarctic. They record temperatures, barometric and humidity readings and wind speeds which have been recorded at 140 miles (225 km) an hour! Ordinary winds of 60 mph (96 kph) can blow snow though a heavy parka. Temperatures as low as -117°F (-82°C) have been recorded at the South Pole.

PROJECT

Make replicas of and learn how to use different recording instruments used in Antarctic weather stations.

DIRECTIONS

1. Review the project directions (following page) and gather all supplies.

2. Place children in pairs or small cooperative groups. Give each pair or group the directions for a weather recording instrument plus the supplies for making it.

3. When experimentation is complete, invite students to share their projects, observations and conclusions with classmates.

MATERIALS

GENERAL SUPPLIES

- Ruler
- Lightweight cardboard
- Paper
- Glue
- Drinking straw
- Marking pens
- Scissors

Barometer

- Balloons
- Baby food jar
- Heavy rubber band

Thermometer

- Modeling clay
- Food color
- Glass bottle

Rain Guage

- Measuring cup
- Liter soda bottle

Wind Vane

- Long tack
- Pencil with eraser
- Compass

BAROMETER

1. Cut open a balloon and stretch it tightly over the mouth of a baby food or similar size jar. Secure with a rubber band. Cut the end of a drinking straw into a point. Glue the other end to the balloon as shown.

2. Fold a piece of cardboard and set it next to the jar. Mark where the pointed end of the straw touches the cardboard. Mark the line with number 5. Make five lines, 3 cm apart, counting down from 5 and five lines counting up from 5. Number the lines 0–10. The straw should point at number 5.

3. Record the readings for one week at the same time every day along with the weather conditions at the time of the reading. What conclusions can be drawn?

WIND VANE

1. Push the sharp end of a pencil through the middle of an inverted paper cup.

2. Cut four small and two large tagboard triangles. Label the small triangles **N,S,E,W**. Fold the wide end down and glue them to the cup.

3. Cut slits in both straw ends and insert the large triangles to make a pointer, called a "vane". Push the tack through the center of the straw and the pencil eraser.

4. Use a compass to position the wind vane and anchor it with clay or tape. Record the changes in the wind's direction.

RAIN GAUGE

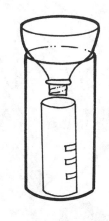

1. Cut off the tops of a liter soda bottle and a smaller clear plastic bottle or jar. Pour ¼ cup (60 ml) water into small jar. Mark the level. Repeat step 2 several times so that you have a series of marks.

2. Empty the small bottle and place it inside the large bottle. Put the top of the large bottle upside down over the small bottle to form a funnel. Set the gauge outside. Record the level of water in the bottle after a rain.

THERMOMETER

1. Fill three-quarters of the bottle with cold water. Add food coloring. Insert the straw so it dips in the water. Seal with modeling clay. Blow gently into the straw stopping when the water level reaches halfway up the straw.

2. Cut two slits in a tagboard square. Slide it over the straw. Mark the level of the water with a pen. Put the thermometer in a warm place. When the water rises, mark the level with a line and the word "warmer". (Heat expands the air and pushes the water up the straw.)

3. Repeat in the refrigerator. When the level falls, mark it with the word "cooler". (The air contracts as it cools, sucking the water back down the straw.)

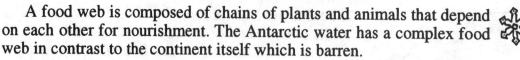

FOOD WEB

HISTORICAL AID

A food web is composed of chains of plants and animals that depend on each other for nourishment. The Antarctic water has a complex food web in contrast to the continent itself which is barren.

The Southern Ocean is rich in nutrients, and tiny plants and animals known as plankton thrive in the cold water. Krill, a shrimplike animal that grows no bigger than 2.5 inches (6.4 cm) eats the tiny plants. Krill is the most important food source in the Antarctic food chain. Sea birds, baleen whales, and seals eat krill. Someday krill may be used as food in many countries.

PROJECT

Learn about how plants and animals depend on each other by making a paper chain that illustrates one part of the Antarctic food web.

DIRECTIONS

1. Reproduce one set of patterns per student.

2. Color and cut out the food chain "links". Form a chain by linking a food source to the animal that eats it.

3. There are many other food chains in the Antarctic food web. For example, a baleen whale eats krill which eats plankton. Research and make a chain that illustrates other Antarctic plants and animals depend on each other.

MATERIALS

• Patterns of food chain "links"
• Scissors
• Crayons or colored pencils
• Tape

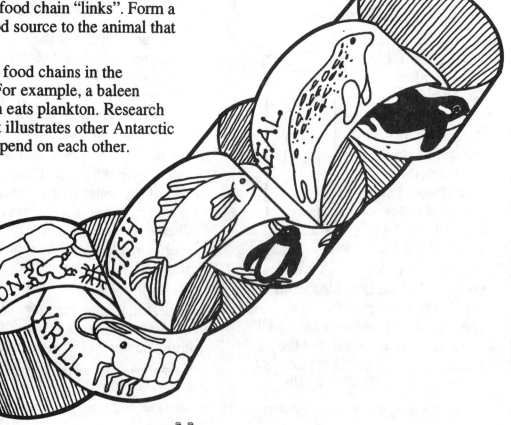

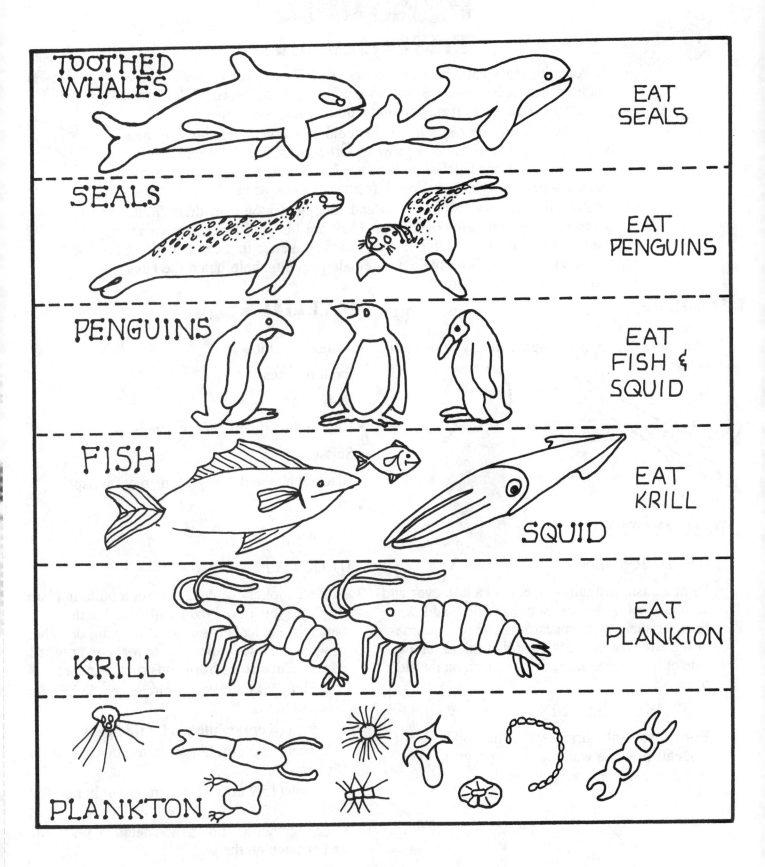

TOOTHED WHALES — EAT SEALS

SEALS — EAT PENGUINS

PENGUINS — EAT FISH & SQUID

FISH — SQUID — EAT KRILL

KRILL — EAT PLANKTON

PLANKTON

PENGUINS
HISTORICAL AID

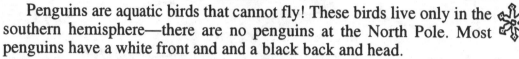

Penguins are aquatic birds that cannot fly! These birds live only in the southern hemisphere—there are no penguins at the North Pole. Most penguins have a white front and and a black back and head.

Of the 17 different species of penguin the largest are the king and emperor penguins which can grow as tall as four feet (120 cm)! Many species have colored patches on their head and neck. Another species, the macaroni penguin, has a yellowish feather crest on its head.

Penguins usually walk or hop and toboggan along on their fronts while pushing with wings and feet. They are fast and agile swimmers. Penguins gather to breed in colonies called rookeries that can consist of thousands of birds. Both male and female penguins help hatch the eggs and care for the baby birds.

PROJECT

Learn about penguins through a variety of penguin activities.

DIRECTIONS

PAINT A PENGUIN

1. Paint a basic penguin shape. Add a bill, eyes and webbed feet. After the paint has dried, add features such as the macaroni penguin's plumes or the emperor penguin's reddish shield on the side of its jaw and large orange patch on the side of its neck.

WALK LIKE A PENGUIN

1. Borrow several pairs of swim fins and have students practice walking like a penguin. You could even have a penguin race!

MATERIALS

- Tempera paint
- Paint brushes
- Swim fins
- Blue and white butcher paper
- Scissors
- Black, white and orange construction paper
- Glue
- Crayons

CUT OUT A PENGUIN

1. Make a rookery of penguins for a bulletin board display. Cover the board with blue butcher paper. Make icebergs with white paint or a sheet of white butcher paper torn to make the ragged edges. Cut circles from construction paper:

   2 inch (5.4 cm) orange circles, cut in half for feet and beaks

   3 inch (8 cm) white circles for heads

   5 inch (13.5 cm) black circles, cut in half for flippers

   6 inch (15.2 cm) white circles cut in half for body

2. Glue together as shown, add details with crayons and arrange on the ice!

WHALES
HISTORICAL AID

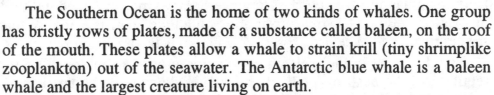

The Southern Ocean is the home of two kinds of whales. One group has bristly rows of plates, made of a substance called baleen, on the roof of the mouth. These plates allow a whale to strain krill (tiny shrimplike zooplankton) out of the seawater. The Antarctic blue whale is a baleen whale and the largest creature living on earth.

The sperm whale is a member of the other kind of Antarctic whale— the kind that have teeth instead of baleen. These whales eat fish and squid and even an occasional penguin.

PROJECT

Mark the length of a blue whale to help imagine the size of the largest animal ever to have lived. The blue whale has been measured up to 100 feet (30.5 m) with a weight of over 220 tons (200 metric tons)!

MATERIALS

• Tape measure
• Playground or large open area

DIRECTIONS

1. Have a student stand where you are going to begin measuring to mark where the blue whale's head would be.

2. Measure 100 (30.5 m) feet and have the students hold hands and stand along the length. Imagine an animal this big!

3. Ask these fun questions:

   How many students could stand in a row on the back of an Antarctic blue whale?

Would a blue whale try to eat you?

How many compact cars weighing 2,400 pounds each would it take to balance a scale that had a blue whale on one side?

What would be the advantages of being the largest creature on earth? What would be the disadvantages?

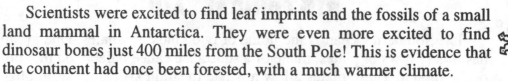

FOSSILS
HISTORICAL AID

Scientists were excited to find leaf imprints and the fossils of a small land mammal in Antarctica. They were even more excited to find dinosaur bones just 400 miles from the South Pole! This is evidence that the continent had once been forested, with a much warmer climate.

The discovery of the skeleton of a Lystosaurus, a 5-foot long (1.5 m) reptile, and the beak of a tall, flightless bird known as the terror bird, were very significant discoveries. Fossils from these creatures had been discovered in other continents. Since neither of these animals were long distance swimmers, their fossil remains in Antarctica is evidence that all the continents were once all connected.

PROJECT

Find out about one of the many ways that fossils were made by making a simulated fossil.

MATERIALS

- Plaster of Paris
- Leaf, bone
- Paper bowls
- Stirring spoon or stick

DIRECTIONS

1. Sprinkle about ½ cup (125 ml) Plaster of Paris into a bowl. Gradually add water, a little at a time, until the plaster resembles uncooked cake batter.

2. Gently press the leaf or other object into the soft plaster. Allow to dry.

3. Research and discuss the various types of fossils.